November 6, 1996

Toni Morrison

THE DANCING MIND

Speech upon Acceptance of the

National Book Foundation Medal

for Distinguished Contribution

to American Letters

on the Sixth of November,

Nineteen Hundred and

Ninety-Six

Alfred A. Knopf · New York · 1996

THE DANCING MIND

There is a certain kind of peace that is not merely the absence of war. It is larger than that. The peace I am thinking of is not at the mercy of history's rule, nor is it a passive surrender to the status quo. The peace I am thinking of is the dance of an open mind when it engages another equally open one—an activity that occurs most naturally, most often in the reading/writing world we live in. Accessible as it is, this particular kind of peace warrants vigilance. The peril it faces comes not from the computers and information highways that raise alarm among book readers, but from unrecognized, more sinister quarters.

I want to tell two little stories— anecdotes really—that circle each other in my mind. They are disparate, unrelated anecdotes with more to distinguish each one from the other than similarities, but they are connected for me in a way that I hope to make clear.

The first I heard third- or fourth-hand, and although I can't vouch for its accuracy, I do have personal knowledge of situations exactly like it. A student at a very very prestigious university said that it was in graduate school while working on his Ph.D. that he had to teach himself a skill he had never learned. He had grown up in an affluent community with very concerned and caring parents. He said that his whole life had been filled with carefully selected activities: educational, cultural, athletic. Every waking hour was filled with events to enhance his life. Can you see him? Captain of his team. Member of the Theatre Club. A Latin Prize winner. Going on vacations designed for pleasure and meaningfulness; on fascinating and educational trips and tours; attending excellent camps along with equally highly motivated peers. He gets the best grades, is a permanent fixture on the honor roll, gets into several of the best universities, graduates, goes on to get a master's degree, and now is enrolled in a Ph.D. program at this first-rate university. And it is there that (at last,

but fortunately) he discovers his dis-
ability: in all those years he had
never learned to sit in a room by himself and read for four hours and have
those four hours followed by another
four without any companionship but
his own mind. He said it was the
hardest thing he ever had to do, but
he taught himself, forced himself to
be alone with a book he was not
assigned to read, a book on which
there was no test. He forced himself
to be alone without the comfort or dis-
turbance of telephone, radio, tele-
vision. To his credit, he learned this
habit, this skill, that once was part of
any literate young person's life.

The second story involves a first-
hand experience. I was in Strasbourg

attending a meeting of a group called the Parliament of Writers. It is an organization of writers committed to the aggressive rescue of persecuted writers. After one of the symposia, just outside the doors of the hall, a woman approached me and asked if I knew anything about the contemporary literature of her country. I said no; I knew nothing of it. We talked a few minutes more. Earlier, while listening to her speak on a panel, I had been awestruck by her articulateness, the ease with which she moved among languages and literatures, her familiarity with histories of nations, histories of criticisms, histories of authors. She knew my work; I knew nothing of hers. We continued to talk, animatedly, and then, in the middle of it, she began to cry. No sobs, no heaving shoulders, just great tears rolling down her face. She did not wipe them away and she did not loosen her gaze. "You have to help us," she said. "You have to help us. They are shooting us down in the street." By "us" she meant women who wrote against the grain. "What can I do?" I asked her. She said, "I don't know, but you have to try. There isn't anybody else."

Both of those stories are comments on the contemporary reading/writing life. In one, a comfortable, young American, a "successfully" educated male, alien in his own company, stunned and hampered by the inadequacy of his fine education, resorts to autodidactic strategies to move outside the surfeit and bounty and excess and (I think) the terror of growing up vacuum-pressured in this country and to learn a very old-fashioned skill. In the other, a splendidly educated woman living in a suffocating regime writes in fear that death may very well be the consequence of doing what I do: as a woman to write and publish unpoliced narrative. The danger of both environments is striking. First, the danger to reading that our busied-up, education-as-horse-race, trophy-driven culture poses even to the entitled; second, the physical danger to writing suffered by persons with enviable educations who live in countries where the practice of mod-

ern art is illegal and subject to official
vigilantism and murder.

I have always doubted and disliked
the therapeutic claims made on be-
half of writing and writers. Writing
never made me happy. Writing never
made me suffer. I have had misfor-
tunes small and large, yet all through
them nothing could keep me from
doing it. And nothing could satiate
my appetite for others who did. What
is so important about this craft that it
dominates me and my colleagues? A
craft that appears solitary but needs
another for its completion. A craft
that signals independence but relies
totally on an industry. It is more than
an urge to make sense or to make
sense artfully or to believe it matters.
It is more than a desire to watch other

writers manage to refigure the world. I know now, more than I ever did (and I always on some level knew it), that I need that intimate, sustained surrender to the company of my own mind while it touches another's—which is reading: what the graduate student taught himself. That I need to offer the fruits of my own imaginative intelligence to another without fear of anything more deadly than disdain—which is writing: what the woman writer fought a whole government to do.

The reader disabled by an absence of solitude; the writer imperiled by the absence of a hospitable community. Both stories fuse and underscore for me the seriousness of the industry whose sole purpose is the publication of writers for readers. It is a business, of course, in which there is feasting, and even some coin; there is drama and high, high spirits. There is celebration and anguish, there are flukes and errors in judgment; there is brilliance and unbridled ego. But that is the costume. Underneath the cut of bright and dazzling cloth, pulsing beneath the jewelry, the life of the book world is quite serious. Its real life is about creating and producing and distributing knowledge; about making it possible for the entitled as well as the dispossessed to experience one's own mind dancing with another's; about making sure that the environment in which this work is done is welcoming, supportive. It is making sure that no encroachment of private wealth, government control, or cultural expediency can interfere with what gets written or published. That no conglomerate or political wing uses its force to still inquiry or to reaffirm rule.

Securing that kind of peace—the peace of the dancing mind—is our work, and, as the woman in Strasbourg said, "There isn't anybody else."

Toni Morrison
November 1996

The Works of Toni Morrison

A Note About the Author

Toni Morrison was born in Ohio and is a graduate of Howard University and Cornell University. She has worked in publishing and taught at various colleges and universities, including Yale, Rutgers, and SUNY Albany as the Schweitzer Chair. She is currently Robert F. Goheen Professor at Princeton. She was the recipient of the 1993 Nobel Prize for Literature.

The text of this book was set in
Bodoni Book, and it was printed by
Berryville Graphics, Berryville, Virginia.
It was designed by Virginia Tan,
based on a design by Peter A. Andersen.